LOST IN THE AMAZON

JULIANE KOEPCKE'S STORY

T0018789

BY BETSY RATHBURN
ILLUSTRATION BY TATE YOTTER
COLOR BY GERARDO SANDOVAL

Black Sheep

BELLWETHER MEDIA • MINNEAPOLIS, MN

STRAY FROM REGULAR READS
WITH BLACK SHEEP BOOKS.
FEEL A RUSH WITH EVERY READ!

This edition first published in 2022 by Bellwether Media, Inc.

No part of this publication may be reproduced in whole or in part without written permission of the publisher.
For information regarding permission, write to Bellwether Media, Inc., Attention: Permissions Department,
6012 Blue Circle Drive, Minnetonka, MN 55343.

Library of Congress Cataloging-in-Publication Data

Names: Rathburn, Betsy, author.
Title: Lost in the Amazon : juliane koepcke's story / by Betsy Rathburn.
Description: Minneapolis, MN : Bellwether Media, Inc., 2022. | Series: True survival stories | Includes bibliographical
    references and index. | Audience: Ages 7-13 | Audience: Grades 4-6 | Summary: "Exciting illustrations follow the story
    of Juliane Koepcke. The combination of brightly colored panels and leveled text is intended for students in grades 3
    through 8"–Provided by publisher.
Identifiers: LCCN 2021025022 (print) | LCCN 2021025023 (ebook) | ISBN 9781644875483 (library binding) |
    ISBN 9781648345043 (paperback) | ISBN 9781648344565 (ebook)
Subjects: LCSH: Koepcke, Juliane–Juvenile literature. | Airplane crash survival–Peru–Juvenile literature. |
    Aircraft accidents–Peru–Juvenile literature.
Classification: LCC TL553.9 .R38 2018 (print) | LCC TL553.9 (ebook) | DDC 363.12/40985–dc23
LC record available at https://lccn.loc.gov/2021025022
LC ebook record available at https://lccn.loc.gov/2021025023

Editor: Christina Leaf   Designer: Andrea Schneider

Printed in the United States of America, North Mankato, MN.

TABLE OF CONTENTS

Red text identifies historical quotes.

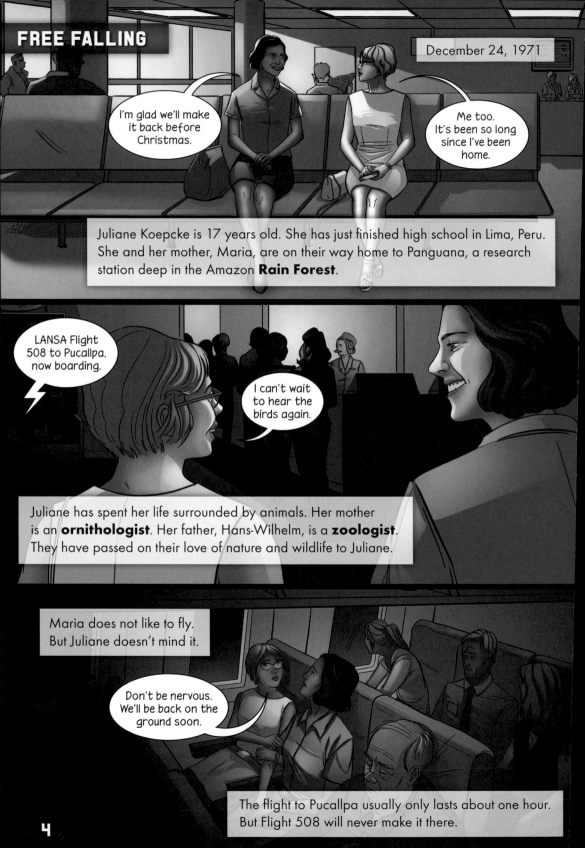

December 24, 1971

I'm glad we'll make it back before Christmas.

Me too. It's been so long since I've been home.

Juliane Koepcke is 17 years old. She has just finished high school in Lima, Peru. She and her mother, Maria, are on their way home to Panguana, a research station deep in the Amazon **Rain Forest**.

LANSA Flight 508 to Pucallpa, now boarding.

I can't wait to hear the birds again.

Juliane has spent her life surrounded by animals. Her mother is an **ornithologist**. Her father, Hans-Wilhelm, is a **zoologist**. They have passed on their love of nature and wildlife to Juliane.

Maria does not like to fly. But Juliane doesn't mind it.

Don't be nervous. We'll be back on the ground soon.

The flight to Pucallpa usually only lasts about one hour. But Flight 508 will never make it there.

About halfway to Pucallpa, the plane runs into a thunderstorm.

Please remain seated. We're experiencing some **turbulence**.

For about 10 minutes, the plane rocks and shakes through the air. Thunder roars while lightning flashes.

Then, a bright flash of lightning strikes the plane.

CRACK!

Now it's all over.

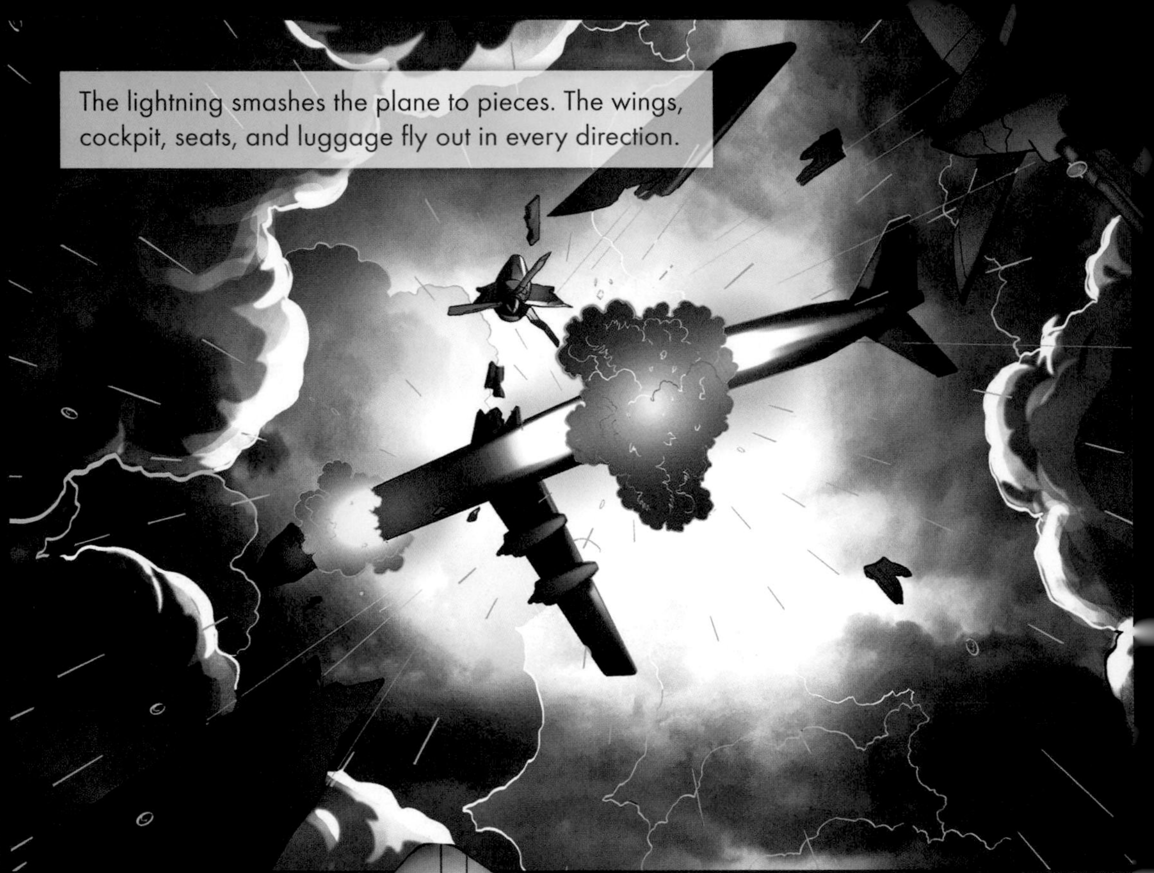
The lightning smashes the plane to pieces. The wings, cockpit, seats, and luggage fly out in every direction.

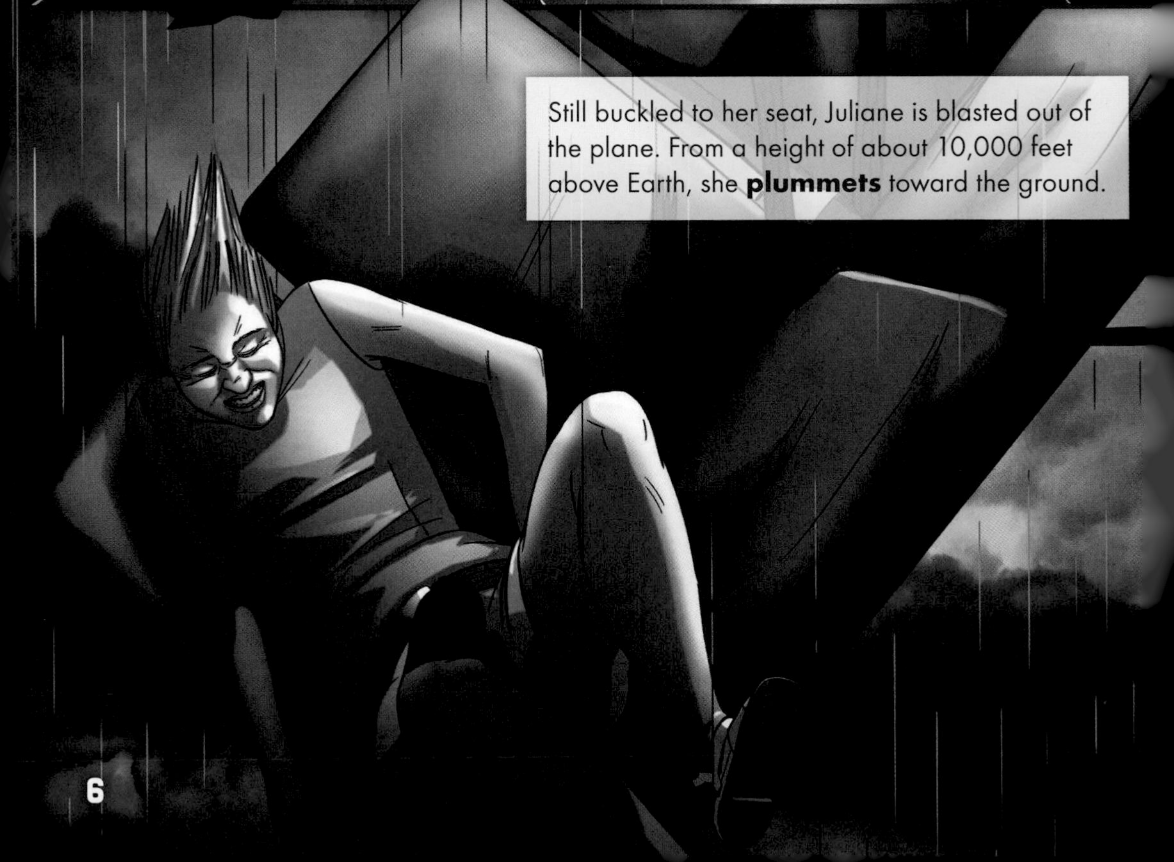
Still buckled to her seat, Juliane is blasted out of the plane. From a height of about 10,000 feet above Earth, she **plummets** toward the ground.

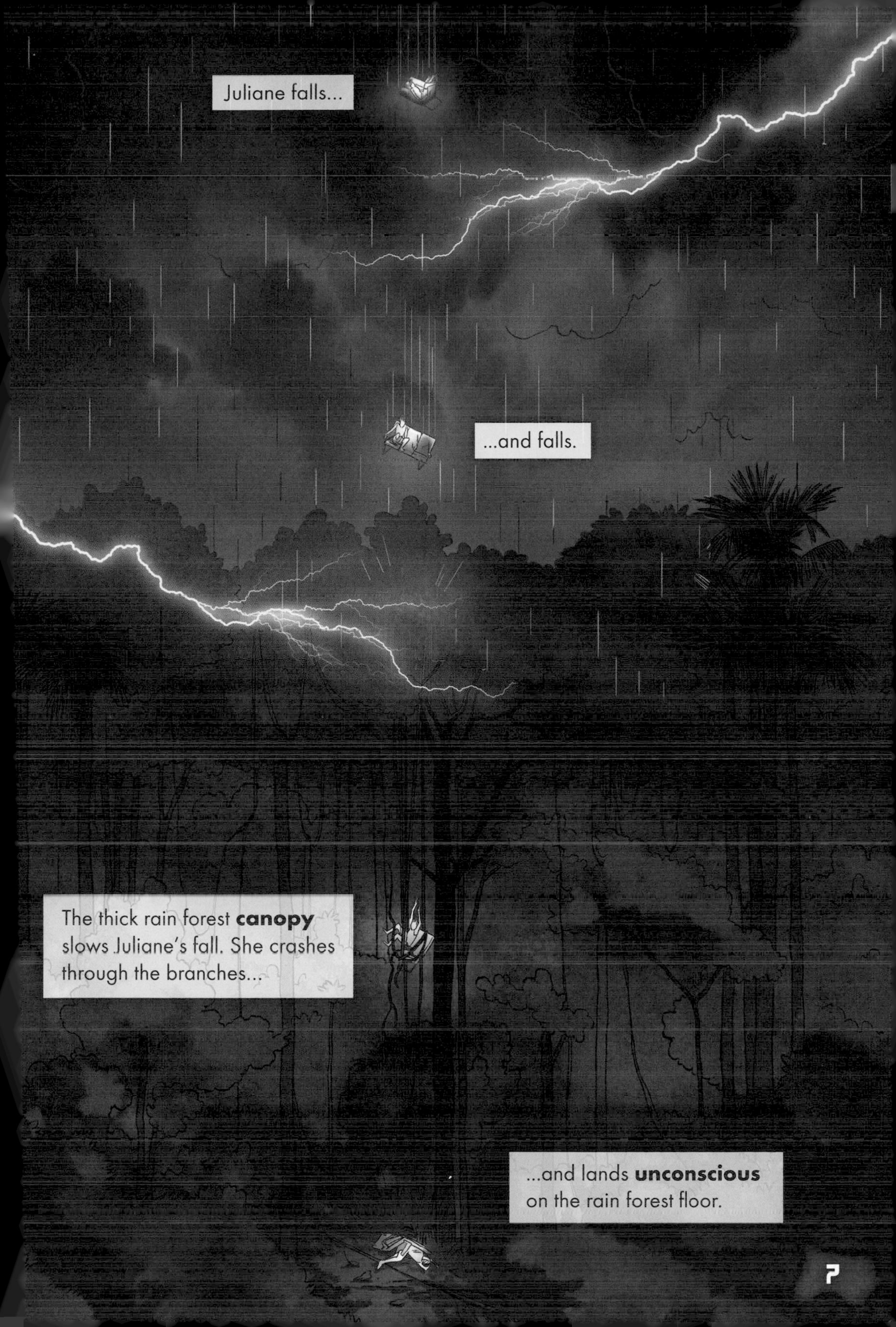
Juliane falls...
...and falls.
The thick rain forest **canopy** slows Juliane's fall. She crashes through the branches...
...and lands **unconscious** on the rain forest floor.

When she wakes up, Juliane is weak. She can barely sit up, but she tries to check her watch.

What time is it? Did that really just happen?

Eventually, Juliane manages to stand.

Hello! Is anyone there?

She searches for her mother and any other passengers. But soon Juliane realizes that she is completely alone.

The only useful item Juliane can find from the crash is a small package of candy.

Juliane hears planes flying overhead. She realizes they must be searching for her flight. But she knows they cannot see her. The forest canopy is too thick.

I have to get moving. If I don't, I may never make it back to Panguana.

As she tries to decide which direction to walk in, Juliane hears a light trickling noise.

WATER!

This stream may lead to a village. Maybe I can find help.

Juliane remembers what her father had taught her. If she followed water, she would eventually find **civilization**.

As she starts off through the rain forest, Juliane thinks about other lessons from her parents. Her memories will help her survive the next 10 days.

ALONE IN THE JUNGLE

Juliane follows the stream for many hours. Because she only has one shoe and can't see well without her glasses, she must be careful not to step on anything dangerous. She feels in front of her with her sandaled foot before taking each step.

She finds a piece of **wreckage** from her flight. It gives her a clue about the damage that was done.

This must be where the lightning struck.

Where are the other passengers?

She also encounters wildlife.

That looks like a bird-eating spider. But it shouldn't hurt me if I stay over here.

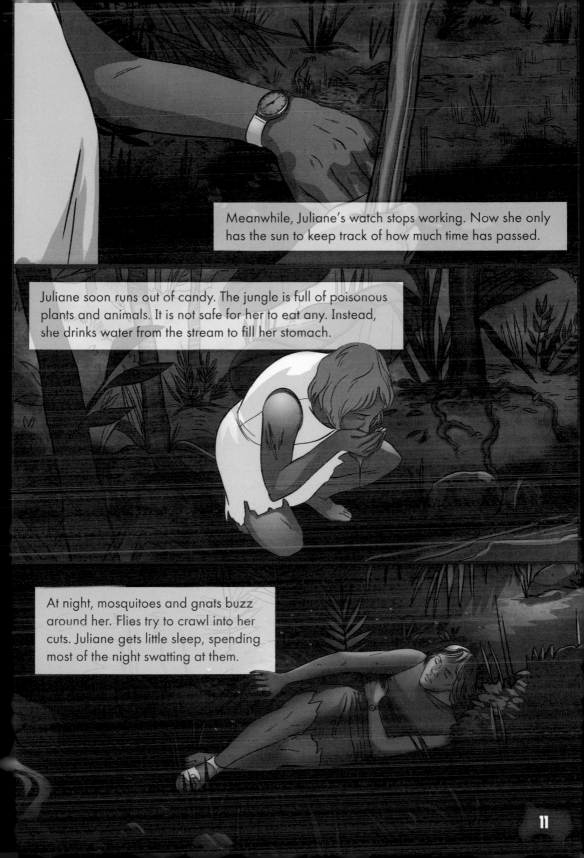

Meanwhile, Juliane's watch stops working. Now she only has the sun to keep track of how much time has passed.

Juliane soon runs out of candy. The jungle is full of poisonous plants and animals. It is not safe for her to eat any. Instead, she drinks water from the stream to fill her stomach.

At night, mosquitoes and gnats buzz around her. Flies try to crawl into her cuts. Juliane gets little sleep, spending most of the night swatting at them.

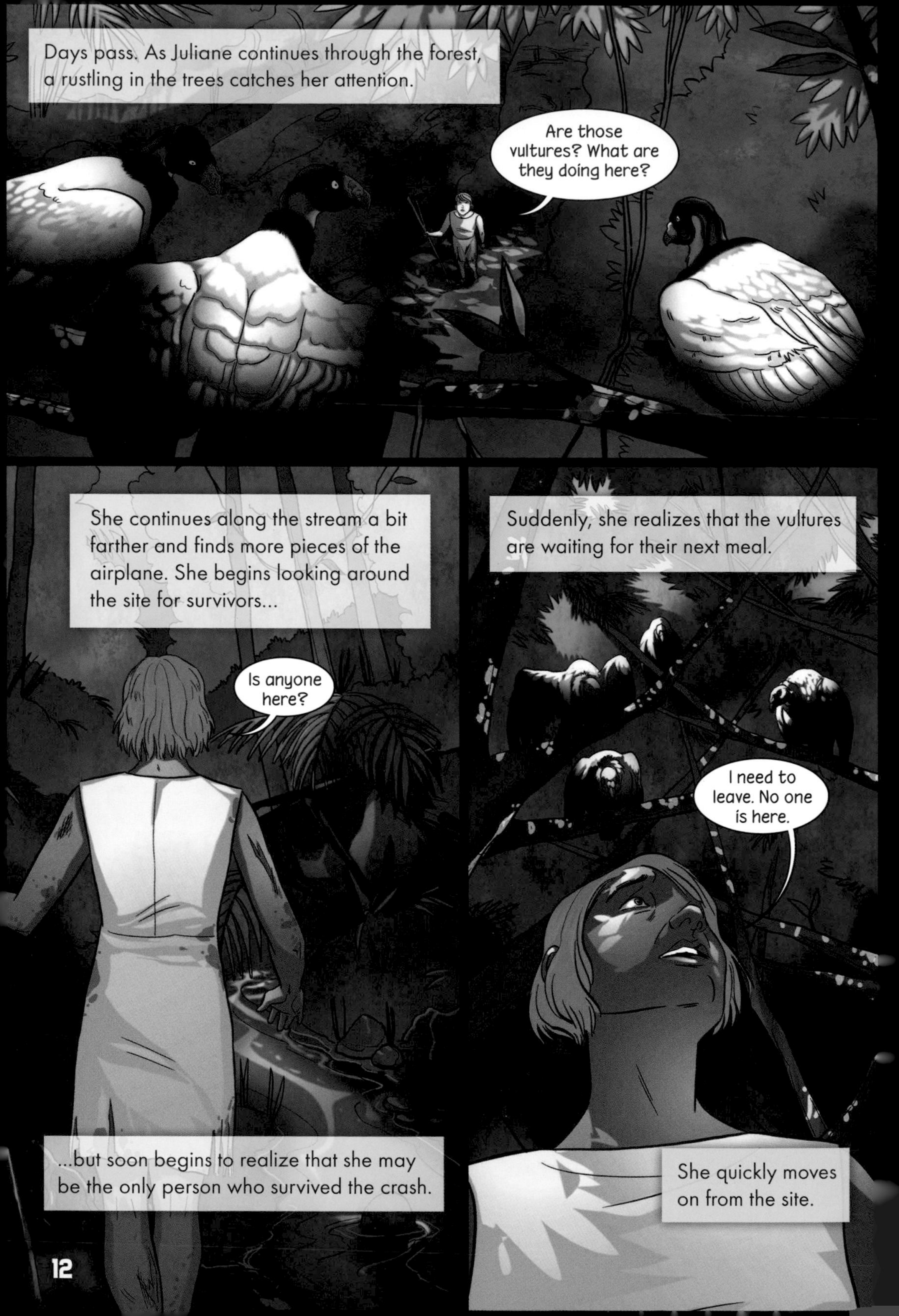

Days pass. As Juliane continues through the forest, a rustling in the trees catches her attention.
Are those vultures? What are they doing here?
She continues along the stream a bit farther and finds more pieces of the airplane. She begins looking around the site for survivors...
Is anyone here?
...but soon begins to realize that she may be the only person who survived the crash.
Suddenly, she realizes that the vultures are waiting for their next meal.
I need to leave. No one is here.
She quickly moves on from the site.

But the vultures are not the only birds Juliane encounters...

HOATZINS!

Juliane has seen many hoatzins at Panguana. She learned a lot about the unusual birds from her mother.

Hoatzins only live near open water, so the stream must open up soon. I'm sure there are people nearby!

The birds give Juliane hope that she will soon be rescued. But her journey is far from over.

Juliane follows the stream until it meets a wide river. But the way is blocked.

Juliane leaves the stream to travel through the jungle. The plants are so thick that it takes hours...

If I can't get over it, I'll have to go around it.

...but she eventually makes it to the Shebonya River.

Finally! But I'll have to be careful. This riverbank is a perfect home for stingrays.

A sting would likely be deadly.

Juliane decides it is better to travel by water. The river is full of danger, too. Piranhas swim there. But Juliane knows they will not harm her in the flowing water.

Caimans and crocodiles also live in the river. Juliane makes sure to steer clear of them

Juliane travels more quickly by water. But she still encounters many **obstacles**. She begins to doubt that any people live nearby.

If people boated in these waters, there wouldn't be so many logs.

But she has no choice but to continue. The jungle is much more dangerous than the water.

FOUND AT LAST

By the tenth day of her journey, Juliane has not eaten in many days. Though she knows they may be poisonous, she tries to catch frogs...

...but she is too slow.

Juliane's hunger makes it difficult to continue her journey. The pain from her wounds is also making her weaker.

With no sign of any people, she begins to lose hope that she will ever find her way out of the rain forest.

As she rests on a riverbank that evening, Juliane notices a strange sight.

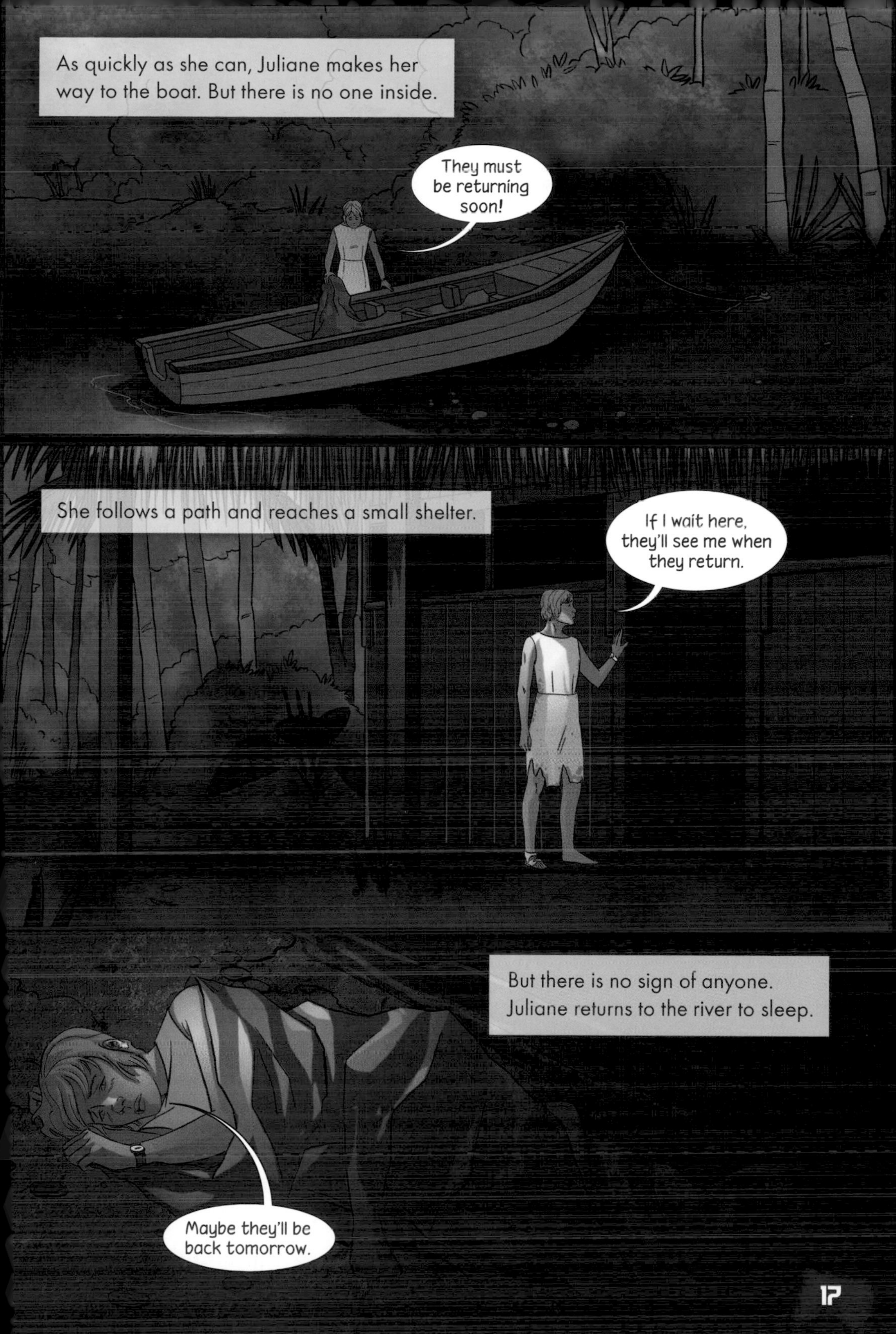
As quickly as she can, Juliane makes her way to the boat. But there is no one inside.
They must be returning soon!
She follows a path and reaches a small shelter.
If I wait here, they'll see me when they return.
But there is no sign of anyone. Juliane returns to the river to sleep.
Maybe they'll be back tomorrow.

Juliane spends the next day at the shelter. Rain forces her to wait inside. There is still no sign of anyone...

...but then she hears a new sound.

I can't stay here forever. If no one comes today, I will leave tomorrow.

Could that be voices?

Three forest workers emerge from the jungle. They are Beltrán Paredes, Carlos Vásquez, and Nestor Amasifuén.

‹I'm a girl who was in the LANSA crash. My name is Juliane.›

< > Translated from Spanish

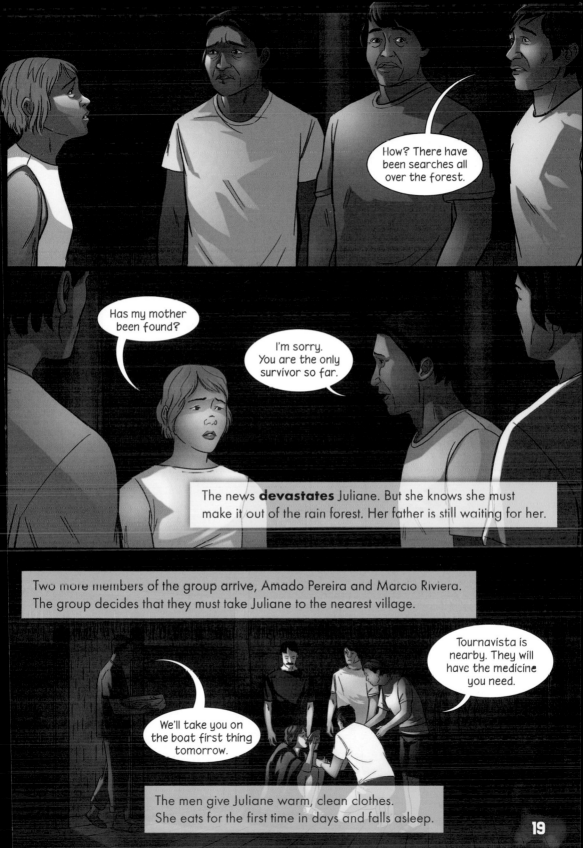

How? There have been searches all over the forest.

Has my mother been found?

I'm sorry. You are the only survivor so far.

The news **devastates** Juliane. But she knows she must make it out of the rain forest. Her father is still waiting for her.

Two more members of the group arrive, Amado Pereira and Marcio Riviera. The group decides that they must take Juliane to the nearest village.

Tournavista is nearby. They will have the medicine you need.

We'll take you on the boat first thing tomorrow.

The men give Juliane warm, clean clothes. She eats for the first time in days and falls asleep.

The next morning, Amado and Marcio help Juliane into the motorboat. She rests while the men steer down the river.

The trip takes many hours.

I never would have made it this far.

Juliane realizes that it would have been impossible to continue without help.

In Tournavista, Juliane is offered a flight to a larger city, Yarinacocha, where she can see a doctor.

Though she is afraid to fly again, this is the fastest way to get the care she needs.

I am so glad you made it back to me.

Me too.

Juliane reunites with her father in Yarinacocha. She spends some time recovering there, and eventually makes it back to Panguana. She is safe and sound at last.

Once she recovered, Juliane left Peru to live in Germany, where her parents were from. For many years, Juliane worked to turn her parents' hard work at Panguana into a permanent **conservation** area. Her dream became a reality in 2011.

Today, Panguana protects the many plants and animals that live around Juliane's childhood home. She never forgot her time in the rain forest!

MORE ABOUT JULIANE KOEPCKE

✛ When she moved to Germany, Juliane studied to become a mammalogist. She now researches mammals in Germany.

✛ During her studies, Juliane focused on researching the bats that live around Panguana. More than 50 types of bats are found there!

✛ In 1998, filmmaker Werner Herzog made a movie about Juliane's survival. They retraced her trip through the rain forest and visited her crash site.

JULIANE KOEPCKE TIMELINE

December 24, 1971
Juliane's plane crashes into the Amazon Rain Forest

around December 29, 1971
Juliane sees hoatzins, causing her to find the Shebonya River

January 4, 1972
Juliane makes it out of the rain forest

December 25, 1971
Juliane begins her journey through the rain forest

January 3, 1972
Juliane is found by forest workers

JULIANE KOEPCKE'S ROUTE

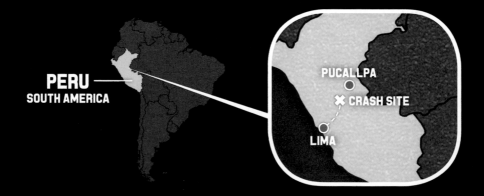

PERU
SOUTH AMERICA

PUCALLPA
✖ CRASH SITE
LIMA

GLOSSARY

canopy—the uppermost layer of branches in the rain forest

civilization—a place where people live that has stores, hospitals, and other necessities

conservation—the planned management of a natural resource to protect it

devastates—brings overwhelming sadness

obstacles—objects that slow or stop movements

ornithologist—a scientist who studies birds

plummets—falls quickly

rain forest—a thick, green forest that receives a lot of rain; rain forests are home to many different plants and animals.

turbulence—quick, irregular movements of air; when an airplane hits turbulence, the ride can be bumpy.

unconscious—not awake, especially because of an injury

wreckage—the broken parts of an object

zoologist—a scientist who studies animals

TO LEARN MORE

AT THE LIBRARY

Klepeis, Alicia Z. *Peru*. Minneapolis, Minn.: Bellwether Media, 2019.

Perish, Patrick. *Survive A Plane Crash*. Minneapolis, Minn.: Bellwether Media, 2017.

Vonder Brink, Tracy. *Protecting the Amazon Rainforest*. Lake Elmo, Minn.: Focus Readers, 2020.

ON THE WEB

FACTSURFER

Factsurfer.com gives you
a safe, fun way to find
more information.

1. Go to www.factsurfer.com
2. Enter "Juliane Koepcke" into the search box and click Q.
3. Select your book cover to see a list of related content.

INDEX